Original title:
Beneath the Tidal Surge

Copyright © 2025 Creative Arts Management OÜ
All rights reserved.

Author: Miriam Kensington
ISBN HARDBACK: 978-1-80587-414-0
ISBN PAPERBACK: 978-1-80587-884-1

A Driftwood's Tale

A piece of wood with stories grand,
Floats all day at the ocean's command.
He sighs of ships that came and went,
And claims he's sailed with a pirate's dent.

The seagulls laugh, they know he's sore,
His only crew, the waves that roar.
"Once I was a tree!" he tells the beach,
But to the tide, he can't quite reach.

Between the Rocks and the Flow

Between the stones, a fish did dance,
In his own bubble, he took a chance.
He wriggled here, he strutted there,
While crabs just stared with vacant glare.

"Oh look at me!" he boasted loud,
Pretending to be the ocean's proud.
But a wave took him for a wild ride,
And off he went, the daring tide.

Siren's Lament

A siren sang with voice so sweet,
Until she tripped on her own two feet.
Splash went her hair, what a sight!
The fish below just roared with delight.

Her songs now humor, not sorrow's ache,
As dolphins giggle from waves they shake.
"Oh, come back, love!" they joke and jeer,
But all she wants is a dry pair of gear.

The Underwater Reverie

In depths where light begins to fade,
A lobster dreams of a grand parade.
He imagines crowns and royal flair,
Yet all he wears is algae and despair.

The coral mocks with colors bright,
As fish swim past, what a sight!
"Next year!" he vows with grumpy glee,
"I'll trade my shell for a fancy spree!"

Underwater Reverie

Fish in tuxedos, having a ball,
Octopus DJ, spinning for all.
Eels in a line, doing the twist,
Seaweed confetti, you don't want to miss.

A crab in a hat is the guest of the year,
Jellyfish glow bright, we cheer and we cheer.
Seahorses dance like they're in a ballet,
Under the waves, it's a party today!

Veils of Mist and Mystery

Mysteries lurk in the bubblegum reef,
Sharks play peek-a-boo, with quite the belief.
A mermaid sings off-key, just for fun,
Starfish doing yoga, under the sun.

Clownfish tell jokes, and get in a huff,
Shells snicker loudly, this is quite tough.
Whales swap tall tales of life in the dark,
While seagulls argue over who's got the spark!

Pulses of the Ocean Floor

Crabs in a conga line, shuffling about,
With tubes of toothpaste their prizes, no doubt.
Clams roll their eyes, they're so very bored,
While plankton's gossip brings laughter aboard.

Anemones tickle, what a silly game,
Pufferfish puff up, it's never the same.
The sea cucumber tries to keep pace,
But who knew the ocean could be such a race?

Dreamscapes of the Sea

Dolphins hold meetings, plotting a prank,
While bubbles are rising, giving a shank.
The corals giggle, in colors so bright,
As they weave tales of the luminous night.

Turtles in shades, with hats tipped just right,
Shimmering scales catch the soft morning light.
Octopuses juggling with flair in their arms,
Life under waves is filled with its charms!

Songs of the Undercurrents

The fish wear ties, oh what a sight,
Dancing in bubbles, they feel so right.
Seahorses strut in a conga line,
Snapping clams chant, it's party time!

Starfish play cards, no hands involved,
Their genderless woes are quite resolved.
The octopus juggles shells and more,
As krill knock on wood to settle the score.

Fathoms of Reflection

Down in the depths, a mermaid sings,
Her tune is lost on remote sea kings.
Turtles roll dice, their fate on a whim,
While eels tell jokes, their humor quite grim.

A crab with a cane thinks he's a lord,
He walks with a swagger, as if he's adored.
A whale texts dolphins, 'Let's swim and cheer!'
But they're too busy scrolling, it's all too weird.

The Color of Deep Water

Blue fish in suits, they swim on by,
Trading old tales as bubbles fly high.
Coral reefs gossip, they're quite well-read,
While plankton whispers, 'Do I need to dread?'

A pufferfish bursts out laughing loud,
As seagulls overhead form a winged crowd.
The tuna play poker, but cheat with a grin,
While jellyfish bob like they're all in!

Shimmering Phantoms

Bubbles of laughter, echo through night,
Ghostly fish waltz in shimmering light.
A squid tries salsa but slips on a floor,
As lanternfish giggle and holler for more.

Anemones daydream, float passing by,
With whims of a party, they reach for the sky.
Sea slugs join in, with their slick, smooth moves,
Chasing their friends in what seems like grooves.

Tides of Tranquility

The ocean's giggle is my delight,
Waves crash and dance, oh what a sight!
Seagulls squawk in comical cheer,
Dodging splashdowns like they're in fear.

Shells tell jokes in the salty spray,
They whisper secrets of the day.
The fish wear sunglasses, truly absurd,
As they frolic beneath each wave's word.

Treasures of the Forgotten Depths

Old boots and bottles, treasures galore,
What once was lost now isn't a bore!
A crab in a top hat struts with flair,
Claiming the junk, as if it's rare.

Mermaids laugh in the watery glow,
Dancing with starfish in a fabulous show.
They've found the old watch that stopped on a whim,
Now it ticks backwards, oh how it swims!

Whirlpools of Memory

In a whirlpool, I lost my hat,
Along with a shoe, and a far-off cat.
Dizzying spins that make you dizzy,
Even the dolphins look all a-fizzy.

Stories get tangled like seaweed in knots,
Tales of a fish who stole my crocs!
The ocean giggles, I must confess,
It's the funniest scene, who could guess?

Nature's Hidden Symphony

The waves play trumpets, the fish do the beat,
As crabs on the shore tap their little feet.
Gulls are the singers, off-key but bright,
Making music from morning 'til night.

Driftwood conducts with a branch in its grip,
While seashells hum along, giving a quip.
In this concert, laughter takes center stage,
Nature's own show, turning each page!

A Symphony of Shells

A clam met a snail on a sandy shore,
They argued about who could dance more.
The crab did a jig, quite the show,
While fish laughed and called it a funny bro.

An octopus joined with eight left feet,
He slipped on a starfish, oh what a feat!
They all laughed hard, their laughter was loud,
At the unexpected dance of their whimsical crowd.

The Hidden Life of Tides

The tides play tricks, like a sneaky cat,
They hide all the treasures, what do you think of that?
A bottle capsized, a message inside,
But it only said, 'I lost my ride!'

A seagull squawked with a voice so bold,
'You want my fries? They're five days old!'
The waves rolled in, with giggles and glee,
As they washed away secrets, so wild and free.

Beneath the Surface Mosaic

Colorful fish wear their scales like a dress,
One tried on a hat, and caused quite a mess!
A turtle swam by, laughing out loud,
'Where's the beach party? I want to be proud!'

The seaweed waved, with a dance of its own,
'Don't mind me, I'm just here to groan.'
They twisted and turned, a colorful spree,
In this underwater ball, everything's free.

Cradle of the Moonlit Sea

The moon looked down, not wanting to sleep,
It saw the waves rise and take a big leap.
A fish took a selfie, posed just right,
While a crab photobombed, what a sight!

Stars twinkled brightly, winking from up high,
As jellyfish floated and wobbled by.
They giggled and jiggled, with laughter and light,
In the cradle of water, everything felt right.

Infinite Blue

In a sea of blue, fish wear hats,
Starfish dance, how odd is that!
Crabs sip tea as waves roll in,
Seagulls gossip about their kin.

Mermaids chuckle, trade their scales,
While dolphins tell the funniest tales.
A whale performs a belly flop,
And everyone laughs till they just can't stop.

Infinite Silence

Silence whispers to the sun,
Even the bubbles have some fun.
They giggle softly, give a tease,
While clams sit tight, just waiting, please.

A turtle wears a snorkel, wink,
And shrimps all join for a drink.
In the quiet, jokes still flow,
Can you hear the ocean's show?

When Waters Embrace the Land

The tide winks at the sandy shore,
"Don't be shy, come dance some more!"
Crabs wear shoes and skip along,
While jellyfish sing a silly song.

As gulls dive-bomb for a snack,
Seaweed joins in, dressed in black.
The waves tickle toes with glee,
Splashing laughter, wild and free!

Reflections of a Drowning Star

A star fell down, quite the sight,
It flailed around, said, "Oh, that's right!"
With fishy friends, it tried to swim,
But all it did was make it grim.

A fish laughed loud, "You can't go far!
Just float and shine, you silly star!"
So they all swam in joyful loops,
Laughing together, the cosmos' goofs.

The Journey of a Wayward Current

A current decided to take a stroll,
With no direction, just like a foal.
It swirled and twirled, went here and there,
Tickling fish with its wild flair.

"Where are we going?" a clam did squeak,
The current laughed, "I'm just a freak!"
So off they dashed toward the deep,
Chasing crabs that couldn't keep.

The Weight of Drifted Echoes

In a sea of lost flip-flops,
Seaweed whispers silly jokes,
Crabs dance to the tide's rhythm,
While fish try on silly cloaks.

A seagull steals a sunhat,
Squawks like a rusty gate,
The oysters make wisecracks,
At sea urchins who contemplate.

Waves toss a beach ball high,
Splashes soak the grumpy whales,
Surfboards giggle on the shore,
As jellyfish tell silly tales.

Starfish count their lucky charms,
While clams play a game of fetch,
The ocean hums a giggly tune,
And seahorses love to sketch.

Cradled by Currents

A rubber duck floats by,
With a crown of seaweed green,
Seahorses play tag under waves,
While clams just want to be seen.

Jellybeans dance in the tide,
Laughing as they trip and twirl,
Octopuses juggle lost keys,
As the sea stars start to whirl.

Drifting past blown-up rafts,
Inflatable sharks in tow,
The waves all wear smiley faces,
A watery circus in flow.

Barnacles tell dad jokes,
As dolphins swear they can sing,
While schools of fish join the fun,
In the currents of unraveling spring.

The Ocean's Hidden Heart

Clams gossip in the sand,
Amusing tales of fishing lore,
Mermaids giggle, wince, and sway,
Each splash brings giggles galore.

A crab wearing shades struts proud,
While a fish plays peek-a-boo,
The waves are laughing uproariously,
With bubbles popping like a boo.

Corals wear party hats,
Inviting all to join the spree,
Anemones get tangled up,
As they dance for crabby glee.

Starfish play a game of chase,
While lobsters share the latest trend,
And sea turtles glide on waves,
Where seamless splashes never end.

Splendor of the Submerged

An old ship's stuck in a laugh,
Turns out a dolphin steers,
Tangled nets make for great capers,
As laughter drowns out all fears.

Clownfish put on silly wigs,
Pretending to be movie stars,
While eels wiggle to the beat,
And turtles strut, oh how bizarre!

Crabs host a crustacean race,
To see who's fastest on the floor,
Fins flip and flippers fly quick,
Splashes mix with wild uproar.

Pearls can't keep a secret, though,
As they gossip with a shell,
The sunbeams laugh above the tides,
In a world where joy excels.

Enigma of the Coral Canvas

In the hues of pink and blue,
Fish wear shoes, how quirky too!
A crab dances, oh what a sight,
While seaweed sways, oh, what a fright!

Turtles giggle with bubbling cheer,
While clams play cards, they shed a tear.
An octopus juggles with great flair,
While dolphins dive without a care!

Remnants of a Drowned Land

Once there stood a towering place,
Now fish swim in a clumsy race.
A sunken chair with barnacles stuck,
And seafoam laughs at its own luck!

A ghost crab tells tales of old,
Of pirate gold and treasure bold.
But the only treasure that remains,
Are shells for pasty, pizza gains!

The Rhythm of the Subaqueous

Bubbles pop in bubbly cheer,
As fish throw parties, all are here.
Anemones dance, waving hello,
While starfish argue on who's the show!

A mermaid croons with a fishy voice,
"Who needs land when we've got choice?"
While sea slugs do the conga line,
Who'd have thought they'd taste divine?

A Tidal Pulse in Time

The tides come in, they bring a joke,
As laughter bursts from every bloke.
A clam jokes 'bout its hidden pearls,
While seahorses giggle and twirl!

The waves wear shells like fancy hats,
All while minnows engage in chats.
A sea cucumber tried a waltz,
But tripped and blamed it on the faults!

Constellations of the Ocean's Heart

In the depths where fishes dance,
Seaweed's twirl gives quite a chance.
A crab in a tux, so refined,
Hoping to impress the shellfish kind.

Stars of the sea, they sparkle wide,
While octopuses try to hide.
With ink in hand, they pen a tale,
Of a dolphin who tried to set sail.

Turtles chasing jelly's float,
Confetti of colors, a playful boat.
A whale with a hat, oh what a sight,
Singing off-key throughout the night.

The waves all giggle, curl, and twist,
As fish debate who'll get the biggest fish.
In this realm where laughter flows,
Every splash ignites the prose.

Driftwood Diaries

A log writes tales of beachside fun,
With barnacles as its number one.
It dreams of days on sandy shores,
While crabs use it for their xylophone scores.

Seagulls squawk, a funny tune,
While starfish ponder 'What's a spoon?'
A tide brought in a squeaky toy,
An octopus tries to play with joy.

Driftwood, bold with stories of old,
Of mermaids who danced when the seas were cold.
A whale spills secrets of fishy dreams,
As starry-eyed guppies swim in teams.

With every wave that comes and goes,
The logs share laughter with seaweed prose.
Each tide's a chapter, a tale to weave,
In driftwood diaries, believe, believe!

Beneath the Foam's Embrace

Amidst the bubbles, fishy curls,
A clownfish wiggles, plays with pearls.
Seahorses dance in a wobbly line,
While crustaceans argue, "Who's more divine?"

The tides bring forth a comedic scene,
With dolphins adding to the marine routine.
A jellyfish winks in vibrant delight,
As mollusks gossip about jellyfish plight.

Bubbles rise, tickling all they meet,
An urchin's prickles, a funny feat.
With tides that stumble and giggles galore,
The ocean's silliness never gets poor.

Chasing shadows in wavy delight,
Clams clamber about, what a silly sight!
Every wave a chuckle from below,
In the foam's embrace, laughter will flow!

Requiem for the Reefs

The reefs convene for a funeral dance,
A fish in a tie leads the bizarre prance.
"Here lies my friend, that knock-kneed crab,
His antics were mad, oh what a fab!"

Corals sob, but with vibrant glee,
"Remember the times he stole a key!"
A lobster reads a soggy old book,
While sea cucumbers just stand and look.

The parrotfish squawks, "Let's not be sad,
He made us giggle, that little lad!"
With shells for trumpets and barnacles drums,
They rock out loud to the music that hums.

As jellyfish bob and sea urchins croon,
A requiem sung in the light of the moon.
For all that's silly, the laughter's a treat,
In the sea of colors, they all take a seat!

The Weight of Water's Silence

The ocean whispers soft and low,
With fishy jokes from depths below.
A crab with glasses starts to read,
While jellyfish swim at lightning speed.

Seashells giggle, tickling sand,
Starfish dance—oh, isn't that grand?
A dolphin flips, makes the waves spray,
Splashing the octopus on his way!

Turtles wear surfboards made of kelp,
They ride the waves, oh what a yelp!
Narwhals joke with their spiral horns,
While seagulls steal the squid's fresh corn.

The weight of water keeps them cool,
As laughter echoes, like a school.
And deep below, in waters vast,
The fishy puns will forever last.

Secrets Carried by the Swell

In the swell of waves, secrets flow,
With whispers of fish in their grand show.
A clam recalls the tale of a shark,
Who thought it a prank, oh what a lark!

The tides tease tales of pirate gold,
But the whispered truth is never bold.
Crabs pass notes on the ocean floor,
While laughing at shrimps who just want more.

An anglerfish fakes a fancy glow,
To impress a squid, but it won't go.
They play a dance in the moonlit night,
Making shadows that give fish a fright!

Secrets swirl with a splashy cheer,
As ocean critters gather near.
With ticklish tides and witty replies,
The swell's deep truth is laughter's guise.

Fragments of an Undersea Dreamscape

In a dreamscape below, where corals bloom,
Bright fish parade, making colors loom.
An octopus paints with ink so sly,
While sea horses laugh as they zoom by.

A treasure chest opened by curious clams,
Filled with lost socks and jelly jams.
A scene unfolds, bizarre yet sweet,
Where turtles gossip and seagulls compete.

Whales sing songs of their lost socks,
While krill form circles, dancing like clocks.
Anemones giggle as they sway back,
And a crab's big hat goes off track!

Dreams drift freely in currents bold,
With laughter echoing, tales retold.
In this magical space, fun won't die,
As fish wear wigs and seaweed ties!

Tales from the Briny Deep

Down in the briny, tales do spin,
Of clowns in gills and grins like fins.
A bottom-feeder starts a show,
With bubbles and winks, oh what a glow!

The sea cucumbers are in disguise,
Making faces, what a surprise!
They tell of crabs in a dance-off scene,
Shuffling sideways, looking quite keen.

Pirate ghosts wear mermaid wigs,
Telling tales with flourishes and jigs.
And schools of fish throw parties bright,
While hammerheads mix drinks by moonlight.

In every wave, a comedy flows,
With punchlines hidden beneath the shows.
So gather round, where the laughter's steep,
And enjoy the tales from the briny deep.

Tribute to the Vanishing Shores

The beach is shrinking, what a sight,
As crabs hold hands in a dance of fright.
Seagulls gossip, sharing the news,
"Hey, there's no room for our boozy snooze!"

The waves keep laughing, just too loud,
While beach balls float like a drifting cloud.
Shells are making their great escape,
"Catch me if you can!" they cheer and gape.

Sunbathers scramble in their chairs,
As the tide tickles toes with cheeky stares.
A towel fortress sways with pride,
But the water's winning this goofy ride!

With every splash, the shoreline sighs,
While flip-flops fly into tangled skies.
The ocean's giggle, a mischievous tease,
Let's all hold on to our sunburned knees!

Where Silence Dances with Shadows

At dusk when the sun gives a goofy grin,
The shadows leap, desperate to join in.
Sandcastles melt, a royal mess,
As crabs waltz by in their fancy dress.

The silence laughs, a panda in disguise,
While moonlit waves do the cha-cha surprise.
Broken flip-flops are doing the jig,
As the ocean whispers, "Oh, my, too big!"

Dolphins dive in a silly bow,
Creating ripples, saying, "Look at us now!"
Starfish clap with their tiny hands,
While sand shrimps throw dance parties on the sands.

And when the night falls, funny and sweet,
The waves still giggle at everyone's feet.
In this silly ballet, let's have some fun,
Where silence prances until the night is done!

The Lament of Lost Shores

Oh, where have all the big waves gone?
They used to trip and tease at dawn.
Now they whisper tales with a shaky grin,
While sandcastles giggle, "We'll take a spin!"

The tide's on a diet, missing its flair,
Algae in the corner, plotting a snare.
"Bring back the splashes, we miss the rush!
Instead we're mushing in this marshy hush!"

Clams are crying for a beachball song,
As the jellyfish jiggles along so wrong.
"Where's the high tide that used to embrace?
We demand a show in this peanut space!"

In nature's circus, there's comedy grand,
With lost little waves holding back their hand.
So here's to the shores that once danced bold,
As we tell their tale with a laugh and uphold!

Whispers of the Deep

In a world where fish wear shoes,
And octopi play peek-a-boo,
The dolphins cheer for jellybeans,
While crabs sing songs of silly scenes.

A turtle sporting funky hats,
Complains of pesky little gnats,
With seaweed salads on their plates,
They throw a party filled with mates.

The Dance of Ebb and Flow

The waves decided they'd do jazz,
With whales in costumes made of pizazz,
The clams would clap, the starfish spin,
As seahorses lost their fins!

Crabby dancers do the crabwalk,
The fish all giggle, it's no small talk,
They splash around in salty bliss,
While sea cucumbers can't help but hiss.

Secrets of the Ocean Floor

On the bottom where the sand is thick,
A grouper plays magician tricks,
He pulls out treasures from a hat,
While dolphins laugh at Mr. Flat.

With clumsy turtles breaking shells,
And snails who write their wishes, spells,
The conch shells gossip, quite absurd,
In whispers only mermaids heard.

Echoes from the Abyss

Down where light is a rare delight,
A pufferfish prepares for flight,
With bubble gum stuck to his nose,
He twirls 'round rocks, and off he goes!

The anglerfish, with its glowing lure,
Plays hide and seek, so demure,
While shrimps get tangled in seaweed chains,
And laugh, "What now? We've lost our brains!"

The Ocean's Embrace

The ocean's hug seems quite absurd,
Dancing crabs that sing, oh so weird.
Seagulls squawk, a vocal brigade,
Splashing waves join the joyful parade.

A jellyfish floats, looking like a fool,
Playing tag with a beach ball, oh what a duel!
Fish in tuxedos swim by with glee,
While starfish clap, dancing on spree.

Clams get clammy, as they giggle aloud,
Waves whisper secrets to the sandy crowd.
It's a circus of life, just a splash away,
Where every tide brings a new cabaret.

So if you're down, come take a dip,
Join the revelry, let go, and skip!
In the ocean's arms, all worries erase,
With laughter and joy, find your own place.

Between Rocks and Waves

Between the rocks, there's a dance so raw,
Crabs do ballet, oh what a flaw!
Seashells giggle, they clap and cheer,
As barnacles nod; "Now that's quite dear!"

A sea-otter slips, looking so slick,
Chasing a fish, oh what a trick!
The waves applaud, a splashy ovation,
In this frothy world of wild rotation.

With sea urchins in bow ties, perched like kings,
They watch the oysters, who start to sing.
"Life's a great joke!" they chorus with zest,
As dolphins flip, showing off their best.

Here's to the tomfoolery that the ocean brings,
With laughter and joy, oh what fun it sings!
In salty air and playful tides,
Life's a comedy, where joy abides.

Secrets Carved in Sand

In the golden sands, secrets do play,
Footprints of laughter washed clean, then sway.
Sandcastles tumble, they wave goodbye,
While gulls watch closely, never shy.

A crab writes love notes, oh what a tease,
While waves erode stories with graceful ease.
Starfish giggle as they miss their cue,
Painting funny shapes in the afternoon blue.

Each grain a whisper of fun and cheer,
As the ocean's laughter echoes near.
With shovels in hand, we dig and dive,
In the playful sand where dreams come alive.

Squishy toes find treasures, both silly and grand,
Finding joy in the toes of this wonderland.
So come, create stories in sandy embrace,
Let's all make memories in this goofy space!

The Depth of Night

When the stars come out, the ocean does wink,
Waves whisper jokes as they swirl and sink.
Moonlit mackerel dance with delight,
While the deep sea chuckles, hidden from sight.

Octopuses juggle with a splash of flair,
Throwing seaweed hats into the air.
Glow-in-the-dark fish strut like a show,
As nocturnal friends join the evening row.

A seal barks laughter, echoing bright,
Beneath the blue waves of the soft moonlight.
The tides giggle softly, tickling the coast,
In this underwater party, we all can boast.

So when the sun sets and the night takes hold,
Dance with the creatures, brave and bold.
In the mystery of night, let your spirit soar,
For the ocean's humor waits, just outside the shore.

Chasing Shadows in the Water

In the splash of a wave, I lose my shoe,
A fish grins wide, like it's laughing too.
Seaweed dances, a tangled mess,
Is that a crab or my dress in distress?

Seagulls caw, they're plotting a feast,
While I slip on a rock, oh dear, what a beast!
Sandy toes wiggle, but I feel so grand,
A mermaid's tail? No, just the ocean's hand.

Buckets and spades, my loyal crew,
Building sandcastles, with a moat anew.
But oh, here comes the tide, what a sly foe,
Wrecking my castle like it's a show!

With laughter and giggles, we dance in the foam,
The waves crash loudly, but we feel at home.
In this silly game of ebb and flow,
Life is quite funny, as the tides come and go.

Echo of the Tidepools

Peeking in puddles where creatures hide,
A starfish grins like it's filled with pride.
The hermit crab scuttles, what's that in his shell?
A treasure map? Or just a shellfish hotel?

Jellyfish float like balloons in the sea,
Bouncing and swaying, so fancy and free.
I try to catch one, but end up with air,
Guess it's not dinner, just a sea-slimy affair!

Tiny fish dart, they're playing a game,
One looks back at me, but it's not quite the same.
I'm the giant here, with shadows so tall,
While they giggle and swim, I can't catch them at all!

In tidepools we find our own little world,
With laughter and joy that's easily swirled.
Each creature a chuckle, each wave a new start,
Echoing laughter fills my salty heart.

Luminescent Whispers

At dusk, the sea glows, a sparkling delight,
I'm tripping on shells, what a comical sight.
Bioluminescent, the creatures parade,
What a wild party, let's get this charade!

A shoal of fish flicker, they're disco balls,
While I leap in the water, the night quickly calls.
Flippers and fins, I'm a sight to behold,
Dancing with sea creatures, all shiny and bold.

Jokes with the octopus, how many can fit?
In this underwater rave, where I do the splits.
A dolphin pops up, with a wink and a grin,
"Hey, human, join in, let's make a big win!"

And in our twilight, the waves take their bow,
As I flail in their rhythm, I think to myself now,
This luminous night, with laughter so bright,
Is the funniest whirlpool in the dim moonlight!

Beneath Waves of Time

A snail's slow race is a sight to behold,
While I plunge in the surf, brave and bold.
Seashells are treasures, or so they say,
But they're just slow whispers from yesterday.

Gulls drop their snacks, what a clumsy affair,
I dodge one pebble, but find myself bare.
Laughter erupts, from the shore to the sea,
With every splash echoing hilarity.

Time takes a break just to watch us play,
As the tides giggle and dance in dismay.
We build forts of sand, a flimsy domain,
A kingdom so silly, brought down by the rain!

With memory-making joy, we dive and we dive,
Each twist and each turn, oh how we thrive.
So here's to the waves, the silly, the fun,
May laughter and tides forever be one!

Sunken Stories

In the depth, the fish do dance,
A shark in a tutu, what a chance!
Octopus makes the best shrimp stew,
With a side of seaweed, just for you!

The clam tells tales of lost desires,
With pearls that shine like campfire fires.
A dolphin rings a comedy show,
With jokes about whales that nobody knows!

Crabs scuttle sideways, plotting a heist,
With sea cucumber as their trusted side-dish.
They plan to steal a treasure chest,
But find only shells, oh what a jest!

Mermaids giggle with shells on their ears,
Mixing potions from laughter and cheers.
They throw seaweed confetti in the air,
Each bubble pops with a whimsical flair!

Lost Treasures of the Sea

A treasure chest beneath the waves,
Holds soggy socks and rubber knaves.
Gold doubloons? Nah, just some shells,
With tales of sea trips and fishy smells.

An old pirate's map, all torn and smeared,
Points to a spot where snacks disappeared!
The fish hold grudges, they laugh at the loot,
'Who needs a treasure when you have a fruit?'

Seagulls squawk, they squabble and argue,
Over stale crackers and a fish-shaped barbecue.
Each wave brings secrets, but they're all quite silly,
Like mermaids doing the hula, oh what a frilly!

Squid writes a novel on kelp leaves,
With ink from jelly, nobody believes.
The real gold? Laughter that ebbs and flows,
In a sea of stories only ocean knows!

Twilight over Coral Kingdoms

As twilight falls on coral reefs,
Clownfish don glasses like coral thieves.
They strut in style, oh what a sight,
With a disco ball of shimmering light!

The sea turtles groove to a reggae beat,
While jellyfish twirl with their stinging feet.
Starfish say, 'We're here in a pinch!'
And do a dance, a floppy flinch.

As the sun dips low, laughter echoes wide,
Even the crabs join the giggly tide.
Under the glow, the seaweed sways,
They prance and dance until the next day.

A conch shell handler spins tales to delight,
Of fishy karaoke under the moonlight.
The deep blue's alive, with joy that sings,
In these coral kingdoms, true happiness springs!

The Abyssal Serenade

In the depths where shadows play,
A snail sings ballads in a quirky way.
With a shell for a mic and a downbeat bass,
The ocean holds concerts, a bubbly embrace!

The angler fish has the best spotlight,
Flashing lights that dazzle at night.
While sea anemones sway with glee,
You won't believe the dance, oh, you just wait and see!

A crab with shades struts down the line,
Swooning the crowd like a true star divine.
With every pinch, the applause gets loud,
As the sea creatures form a silly crowd!

From the depths where the laughter does bloom,
They celebrate life in the ocean's room.
Funny tales in a melodic swirl,
The abyss resounds with a chuckling whirl!

Currents of Forgotten Dreams

In a sea of socks, they swim with glee,
Lost to the depths, where could they be?
Sharks have their snacks; the dolphins just laugh,
While mermaids are knitting a cozy craft.

A clam with a pearl thinks he's quite the star,
Telling tall tales of a sunken car.
The fish roll their eyes, 'Oh please, not again,'
As waves crash in laughter; it's chaos, my friend.

A starfish forgets where it left its keys,
It's stuck in a dance with a colony of bees.
Jellyfish, they jiggle with squid in tow,
Creating a spectacle, putting on a show.

So if you should wander near the brine,
Watch out for the sea donkeys drinking wine.
For under the froth, the humor's quite clear,
In the bubbles and giggles, you'll find treasure here.

Shadows in the Saltwater

The octopus juggles with great delight,
Chuckling at fish in a slapstick fight.
A shoal of sardines performs a quick flick,
While a crab makes a joke, oh so quick!

Seahorses prance in a ballet of sorts,
As sea turtles spin, holding court with theorts.
The shadows dance lightly beneath the blue,
Creating a spectacle for all of the crew.

A conch shell is blown, making everyone jump,
As a rogue wave arrives with a loud, goofy thump.
The seaweed sways like it's caught in a trance,
While anemones wiggle, inviting a dance.

A clownfish grumbles, "Why's the sea so salty?"
As bubbles arise, swirling in folly.
In this world of mirth, laughter will start,
For shadows in water hold the joys of the heart.

The Silent Song of Waves

The waves whisper secrets as they roll ashore,
While sea gulls squawk loudly, demanding more.
A hermit crab hums an off-key tune,
As a beluga groans, 'Not now, it's too soon!'

Seashells gather round for a quiet retreat,
Dancing and twirling on soft, sandy feet.
A sea cucumber joins for a moment of fame,
Singing loud praises, though it's quite lame.

With rhythms of bubbles and glimmers of light,
Sea stars clap slowly, embracing the night.
Yet a fish with a hat won't let silence reign,
Turning tides into concert, 'Let's hear it again!'

So listen, my friend, to the giggles and sighs,
The ocean's a chorus beneath sprawling skies.
In the silent song, there's a raucous delight,
As the waves join the laughter, sparkling and bright.

Depths of a Submerged Heart

In the ocean's embrace, a heart starts to sink,
Chasing its dreams with a curious wink.
Fish wear their best, sequins and lace,
Preparing for parties in the deep sea place.

An anglerfish shows off its light with great flair,
While all the big fish stop and stare.
The rhythm of currents whispers sweet jokes,
As schools of small minnows ignite with pokes.

Crabs are the judges in this wild game,
Each joke shared louder, none is the same.
A whale clears its throat with a rumbling sound,
Dropping punchlines that echo around.

Yet down in the depths, where the shadows play,
Laughter bounces high, chasing gloom away.
So don't underestimate the smile of the sea,
For hearts that are submerged love to giggle with glee.

Voices from the Depths

Fish gossip in bubbles, quite the chatter,
Octopuses fidget, making things scatter.
Crabs tell tall tales, perched on their thrones,
While sea turtles roll their eyes with groans.

With seashells for phones, they ring each other,
'You won't believe me!' says Sister and Brother.
Starfish play poker, but they never fold,
The squids pull their pranks, ever so bold.

Shrimp dance the night away, on the sea floor,
While dolphins practice their stand-up galore.
'What did the coral say to the reef?'
'Stop clowning around, it's causing me grief!'

So next time you're swimming, take heed of the sound,
The ocean's alive, with laughter abound.
Listen closely, it's better than plight,
Just avoid bad jokes; they might cause a fright.

The Secrets the Sea Holds

The jellyfish waltz, twirling with glee,
'Underwater's the place! Come dance with me!'
Clams hide their pearls, calling them precious,
But all they do is look far too suspicious.

Barnacles grumble, stuck to their spots,
'We're not too lazy, just in big knots!'
The seahorses gossip, tails all entwined,
Whispering secrets, two of a kind.

Sardines form circles, all tight and discreet,
Thinking they're clever, they're easy to beat.
A shark pops on by, with a joke on his lips,
'Why don't you school? You'll trip on your flips!'

In this watery world, there's much to explore,
From seaweed's wise wisdom to crabs galore.
So if you dive down, wear your best grin,
For the secrets of sea are buried within.

Anemones and Apparitions

Anemones wave, twirling bright and spry,
'We're the party poopers, come join, oh my!'
Ghostly fish giggle, with a flick of their fins,
'We're all just floating, come join in our sins!'

A mermaid complains, 'I lost my best shell!'
While sea snails tease her, 'You'll find it, oh well!'
The mermen surf noodles, like surfboards they ride,
Catching the currents, oh what a wild tide!

The seaweed sings tunes, both catchy and weird,
While the flounders look on, and they hoot, then they jeered.
'Why so glum, my fishy friend from afar?'
'Just searching for snacks, my mom's lost her car!'

So dance with the spirits, in laughter let's dive,
In the ocean's embrace, our giggles will thrive.
With all its oddities, we take in the spree,
In this world of whimsy, you're a fish, come and be!

Wraiths in the Water

Wraiths swim around, with a flick of their tails,
'Tell me a story!' they beg, without fails.
An old fish grumbles, 'I've got one for you,'
'But first, bring the snacks; we're all feeling blue!'

Ghostly jellyfish muse, 'What's the best trick?'
A seagull overhead plops down with a kick.
'Heard the one about the crab at the bar?'
'They couldn't buy drinks; they've lost all their car!'

The crabs hold a meeting, conspiracies flow,
'Are we all just actors in this watery show?'
With a wink and a splash, they dance between rocks,
While tiny shrimp chuckle, wearing funny socks.

So next time you're wandering near the deep blue,
Think of the wraiths and the laughter they brew.
For life in the ocean's a whimsical ride,
With stories and giggles, in the current, we glide.

Magnetic Murmurs of the Deep

A fish wearing glasses swims with flair,
While squid play chess without a care.
Crabs tap dance on shells, quite a sight,
As dolphins giggle, oh what a delight!

Bubbles pop like jokes in the blue,
Sea turtles joke, "You're looking like stew!"
With seaweed wigs, they strut and preen,
The ocean's stage, where laughter is seen.

Starfish argue who's the best at chill,
Their arms all waving, it's quite the thrill.
A whale sings a tune that's off by a note,
While an octopus plays the piano, remote!

Jellyfish waltz, with a graceful twitch,
Invisible fish tease, which makes them itch.
"Let's throw a party!" the sea calls out,
As anemones giggle, with no doubt!

The Cores of Seaweed Dreams

In a kelp forest, mermaids throw shade,
While clams debate the best beachfront parade.
A seahorse in sneakers tries to race,
But the snails just laugh as they slow down the pace.

Eels in tuxedos get ready to dance,
As crabs do the cha-cha, oh what a chance!
The bubbles rise up, a fish's new song,
"Join the conga!" they say, all day long!

Waves wear a hat, quite dapper and neat,
While barnacles tell tales of the tide's heartbeat.
A giant clam shows off its pearl of a grin,
Playing hide and seek, it's where laughs begin!

In this world where silliness reigns true,
Octopuses juggle with endless view.
The ocean's a theater, full of fun,
Where every creature shines like the sun!

Soliloquy of the Sea

With a wink and a wave, the sea starts its tale,
As dolphins pretend they're on a grand sail.
A walrus sharing jokes, so profound,
As a clownfish rolls in laughter, unbound.

"The tide should be ticklish," says one fish with glee,
While others debate what's for lunch; "not me!"
Seashells gossip about the latest scoop,
Bragging about how they're the best beach group.

A shark in a tux, declaring it's fishy,
While sea cucumbers look rather squishy.
With a splash and a giggle, they dance all around,
Creating bubbles of laughter, such joy found!

The rhythm of waves is a humorous song,
Where even the sea urchins join in along.
As tides lift their chorus, they sing out with glee,
Every creature agrees, the sea's funny!

Glistening Worlds in the Abyss

In the hidden depths, fish rave and shout,
Playing tag with the darkness, no hint of doubt.
A grinning sunfish steals a coral crown,
While starry skies twinkle, never a frown.

Crabs wear capes, feeling like kings,
As glowworms sparkle, doing their flings.
A shrimp with a megaphone shouts out cheer,
"Join our disco!" all creatures draw near.

An anglerfish lights up the dance floor bright,
As octopuses spin, twirling with might.
The creatures all laugh, in joy they rejoice,
Echoing laughter, the ocean's own voice.

With treasures of fun in the depths they roam,
Building castles of laughter, far away from home.
In glistening worlds, mischief's delight,
The abyss sparkles with humor at night!